P9-DWG-275

Dear Parent:

Congratulations! Your child is taking the first steps on an exciting journey. The destination? Independent reading!

STEP INTO READING® will help your child get there. The program offers five steps to reading success. Each step includes fun stories and colorful art. There are also Step into Reading Sticker Books, Step into Reading Math Readers, Step into Reading Phonics Readers, Step into Reading Write-In Readers, and Step into Reading Phonics Boxed Sets—a complete literacy program with something for every child.

Learning to Read, Step by Step!

Ready to Read   Preschool–Kindergarten
• big type and easy words • rhyme and rhythm • picture clues
For children who know the alphabet and are eager to begin reading.

Reading with Help   Preschool–Grade 1
• basic vocabulary • short sentences • simple stories
For children who recognize familiar words and sound out new words with help.

Reading on Your Own   Grades 1–3
• engaging characters • easy-to-follow plots • popular topics
For children who are ready to read on their own.

Reading Paragraphs   Grades 2–3
• challenging vocabulary • short paragraphs • exciting stories
For newly independent readers who read simple sentences with confidence.

Ready for Chapters   Grades 2–4
• chapters • longer paragraphs • full-color art
For children who want to take the plunge into chapter books but still like colorful pictures.

STEP INTO READING® is designed to give every child a successful reading experience. The grade levels are only guides. Children can progress through the steps at their own speed, developing confidence in their reading, no matter what their grade.

Remember, a lifetime love of reading starts with a single step!

In memory of Beatrice,
my favorite chicken
—S.H.

Text copyright © 2013 by Sandra Horning
Cover art and interior illustrations copyright © 2013 by Jon Goodell

Published in the United States by Random House Children's Books, a division of Random House, Inc., New York.

Step into Reading, Random House, and the Random House colophon are registered trademarks of Random House, Inc.

Visit us on the Web!
StepIntoReading.com
randomhouse.com/kids

Educators and librarians, for a variety of teaching tools, visit us at
RHTeachersLibrarians.com

Library of Congress Cataloging-in-Publication Data
Horning, Sandra.
Chicks! / by Sandra Horning ; illustrated by Jon Goodell.
   p.   cm. — (Step into Reading. Step 1)
Summary: A family learns about raising chickens when they buy baby chicks from a local farm.
ISBN 978-0-307-93221-1 (trade) — ISBN 978-0-375-97117-4 (lib. bdg.)
— ISBN 978-0-375-98114-2 (ebook)
[1. Chickens—Fiction. 2. Animals—Infancy—Fiction.] I. Goodell, Jon, ill. II. Title.
PZ7.H7867Ch 2013
[E]—dc23   2011050438

Printed in the United States of America
10 9 8 7 6 5 4 3 2

STEP INTO READING®

STEP 1

Chicks!

by Sandra Horning
illustrated by Jon Goodell

Random House 🏠 New York

We drive to a farm.

We buy chicks.

The chicks go
for a car ride.

Soon we are home.

The chicks are
small and soft.

They chirp and chirp.

We put the chicks
in a brooder.

They need water and
food in their new home.

The brooder has a light.
The light keeps the
chicks warm.

The chicks grow . . .

. . . and grow.

They grow
new feathers.

The chicks can fly
out of the brooder.

We build a coop outside.

The chicks move in.

They grow some more.

The chicks
grow combs
and wattles.

Their beaks
grow bigger.

Their feathers
grow fuller.

Now they are chickens.

We build nest boxes.

The chickens
cluck and cluck.

Some of the
chickens lay eggs.

Now we have
chickens
and eggs!

Soon we will have
chicks again.